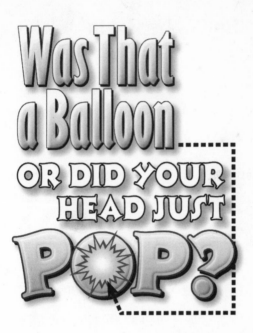

Books by Kevin Johnson

Early Teen Devotionals

Can I Be a Christian Without Being Weird?

Could Someone Wake Me Up Before I Drool on the Desk?

Does Anybody Know What Planet My Parents Are From?

So Who Says I Have to Act My Age?

Was That a Balloon or Did Your Head Just Pop?

Who Should I Listen To?

Why Can't My Life Be a Summer Vacation?

Why Is God Looking for Friends?

Books for Teens

Catch the Wave!

Find Your Fit†

Look Who's Toast Now!

What's With the Dudes at the Door?*

For a free youth missions trip curriculum—or to find out
more about Kevin Johnson's books—visit his Web site:
www.thewave.org

*with James White   †with Jane Kise

Was That a Balloon

Lettin' the air out of popularity bubbles & peer fear

OR DID YOUR HEAD JUST POP?

Kevin Johnson

BETHANY HOUSE PUBLISHERS
MINNEAPOLIS, MINNESOTA 55438

Published by Bethany House Publishers
A Ministry of Bethany Fellowship International
11400 Hampshire Avenue South
Minneapolis, Minnesota 55438
www.bethanyhouse.com

Printed in the United States of America by
Bethany Press International, Minneapolis, Minnesota 55438

ISBN 1–55661–417–9

To Nate, Karin, and Elise

May you always seek popularity

with God.

KEVIN JOHNSON is executive director of Family Hope Institute, a division of Family Hope Services in Plymouth, Minnesota, providing tools and training for people who work with hurting youth and families. He also served as senior editor for adult nonfiction at Bethany House Publishers and pastored a cool group of more than 400 sixth through ninth graders at Elmbrook Church in metro Milwaukee. While his training includes an M.Div. from fuller Theological Seminary and a B.A. in English and Print Journalism from the University of Wisconsin–River Falls, his current interests include cycling, guitar, and shortwave radio. Kevin and his wife, Lyn, live in Minnesota with their three children—Nate, Karin, and Elise.

CONTENTS

CRUSHED BY
THE CAVEMEN

You skip down the hall, joyful to be a seventh grader—gleeful to be back at school after summer vacation. Well, you don't really skip. And you're not quite joyful or gleeful. But you mind your own business, shuffling from class to class, studying your schedule, gliding with a glut of people down the center of the hallway.

Suddenly you feel a hand on each elbow—and another hand around each bicep—and your feet lift off the floor as your back slams against the wall. You hang against lockers, feet dangling. You've been hoisted.

You look to the left. You're held up by a square-headed brute, the human equivalent of one of those Stone Age coelacanth fish everyone thought had died off until they got caught in a fisherman's net off the shore of Africa. On the right you've got Squarehead's thin twin. Only weasely. Wiry. With half a moustache.

"We're the Punishers," Squarehead informs you. "It's our job to remind you that this is *our* school. You twerps don't belong. You better watch yourself. Because we're watching you. You're in our space. We're going to be in your face."

As you sit in your desk next period, you wonder if the prehistoric poets will mess with you again.

It had nothing to do with me, you try to calm yourself. *They were just looking for someone to pick on. They'll leave me alone.* But you decide to dodge them by going down another hallway, just to be sure.

Until you find your way in a school, you get picked up, shaken down, kicked around. You might get your books dumped, your nose tweaked, and the good stuff swiped off your lunch plate.

But what the big old cavemen roaming the halls of life can do to you is nothing compared to the cruelty your peers can dish out. You'd sooner get your head slammed than get slammed by someone you think is your friend.

Sticks and stones break bones.

But being called names hurts worse.

The cavemen of life threaten your body.

People closer to your own size beat up your heart.

It's like this: You're minding your own business when suddenly your life turns into a popularity contest. Everybody votes. And vote after vote, it seems like only a few popular kids come out winners. Their heads inflate to three times their normal size.

Or you might have peers telling you who you're supposed to be—trying to persuade you what you're supposed to like, say, wear. Sometimes they pressure you to be someone you don't want to be. Sometimes they push you places you know you shouldn't go.

Or you might rule your school—public school, Christian school, school-at-home. You're on the dishin' out end. You're the one who tallies the votes in the popularity contest, and you always win. You might feel safe—for now. But sooner or later, life will launch you into situations where you're hoisted. Where you feel socially expendable. Excludable. Beatupable. Pusharoundable.

This book will tell you how to stick a pin in popularity bubbles. How to deflate fear of your peers. How to be the kind of person people want to be around. And how to let God—your Ultimate Friend—into your life.

To use this book, have a Bible nearby that's easy to read so you can look up the passages where it says ✒ **Read.** (Don't blast past those!) To learn even more, you can check the Bible verses that show up here and there in parentheses. And pick some Bible passages and stick them in your long-term memory.

Whoever you are, you're not stealing space on this planet. You belong. You have a right to exist. To breathe, to eat, to bond, to wind your way through the hallways of life, proud of who God made you. But you can't rearrange your life to detour around popularity contests and pushy peers. You need God to get you through. Here's how to grab hold of Him.

2

CHAT CHAT, BLAH BLAH

Jay Leno leans over to pop the question everyone wants you to answer: "So," says talk show Jay, "what's it like being the most popular teen in the world?"

"Tough." You wink. "Been training for years. And it's like climbing Mount Everest. I knew if I wanted to scramble to the top, I needed the right stuff.

"Actually," you continue, "I've got everything I needed in a bag right here." You dig in your book bag. "Look—my last IQ test— 140. Genius, you know. You'd have to be stupid to think you don't need brains. Just be careful not to show 'em. And here's my club membership. I've got sculpted muscles swathed in just-right body fat. Hmm, then some other stuff: flawless clothes, hair, teeth. Oh—and I always carry a few ugly admirers to make me look good."

You rummage at the bottom. "But here's my coolest tool, Jay. It's an attitude I couldn't have gotten along without: I'll do *anything* to be liked by everybody."

📖 **Read Matthew 21:1–11. How did Jesus react when the crowds admired Him?**

People probably don't lay palm fronds in your path and shout "Hosanna! You the King!" Then again, since you're not God's Son, you probably don't expect the royal treatment Jesus got on Palm Sunday.

Still, you've been told what it takes to survive the high winds, frigid cold, and lack of oxygen as you scramble to the top of Mount Popularity. People promise that big biceps or the right bra size or bowing to the crowd's wishes will make you likeable.

Those things won't take you to the top. And they won't keep you on top.

What you don't see in the Bible passage you read is how quickly the fans who crowned Jesus "Mr. Jerusalem" changed their minds. Five days later the people who praised Jesus became a pack of piranhas. They begged He be killed on a cross (Matthew 27:22–23).

Jesus knew that popularity scatters like snow flurries in a mountain wind. So He didn't play to the crowd. Instead, He made obeying God His ultimate aim (John 4:34). Jesus didn't pack for the popularity climb. He picked a path to please God.

————

A very large crowd spread their cloaks on the road, while others cut branches from the trees and spread them on the road. The crowds that went ahead of him and those that followed shouted, "Hosanna to the Son of David!"

MATTHEW 21:8–9

16

A DOG ATE MY ARM

We get voted 'Cutest Couple' at Fall Fest," Tasha fumes, "and then he dumps me! He says he likes Nikki better. And he tells the whole school I'm a 'psychowoman.' Arrgh! I'll show him psychowoman, all right."

"Arrgh," adds Mary Beth.

"And then he thinks I should like him again after *he* gets ditched," Tasha laughs. "Well, now *he* looks pitiful in front of everyone. Why should I care? Too bad!"

"You're too right," Mary Beth chimes. "Too bad."

"He's such a dog!" Tasha wails.

"Totally," Mary Beth agrees. "He's such a dog."

"It's like he bit me bad," Tasha sneers. "He chomped off my arm, then ran down the street with it dangling from his mouth. He's been curled up under a porch somewhere gnawing on the bloody stump—and now he wants to shake my hand."

☞ **Read Galatians 5:14–15. What happens when people battle for popularity?**

When you get caught up in *who-likes-whom* and *who-wins-what* and *who's-better-than-whom*, sooner or later you get clawed. Rubbing shoulders with some folks leaves you feeling ripped off. A few people, in fact, will bite off your other arm if you aren't looking. And watch out: Once they're done with your arms, they'll knock you over and gnaw on your legs.

Lots of people think life is a popularity contest. The battle to be the best is so huge it seems normal. But in God's way of doing things, love is the law.

It's stupid not to realize some people are poised to bite you as they claw their way to the top. It's foolish not to know that a few are so dangerous to your heart that you'd better scamper away when you see them coming (2 Timothy 3:2–5). But to love one another—that's the goal.

Being kinder and gentler may still feel weird.

Then again, what's really weird is gnawing on arms and legs.

When people fight to be popular, both sides wind up bit. And they devour each other down to the last bite.

———————

If you keep on biting and devouring each other, watch out or you will be destroyed by each other.

GALATIANS 5:15

BOTTOM FEEDERS

Josh jumps up and down on the soccer field, pretending to warm up. Actually, he's checking his fan club. One glance and girls on the sideline wave and blow kisses. *This is so cool,* he thinks. *I've got groupies.*

Last season Josh was lousy. Then he grew six inches. And when Josh and the other forwards thrashed his school's archenemy team, he grew a fan club.

Josh tells himself the girls know quality when they see it. After all, they all play, too. He isn't the only guy with a cheerleading section. And hey, Josh is no sexist pig. The guys go and cheer at the girls' games, too.

Josh's parents, though, are less than thrilled with his new friends, both guys and girls. Sure, they smell drug-free. But they constantly sass one another and slam everyone else. Josh's parents suggest he hang out with his old church friends. But who needs them when he has half the girls' team after him?

☞ **Read Proverbs 13:20. Why hang out with wise guys—and gals?**

Get this one: Whole species of scavenging fish have figured out that there's always plenty of food if you're willing to suck lake-bottom muck.

Get this two: You'll always have lots of friends if you settle for less-than-best.

Get this three: Less-than-best may be even less than you think.

The Bible shows two kinds of wise guys and gals: James says that *real wise guys* are "pure; then peace-loving, considerate, submissive, full of mercy and good fruit, impartial and sincere." They live a "good life" full of "deeds done in the humility that comes from wisdom."

The scoop on *fake wise guys* is scary. James says that when people are full of "bitter envy and selfish ambition," life is full of "disorder and every evil practice." And a little bit of fake wisdom gets hugely nasty: it's "earthly, unspiritual, of the devil" (James 3:13–17).

Got it? Friends that seem "not so bad" can be really "not good at all."

You can be a bottom-feeder and grow bloated on cruddy friends. Or you can look for the best friends.

You are what you eat.

———————

He who walks with the wise grows wise, but a
companion of fools suffers harm.

PROVERBS 13:20

5

SCRAPE AWAY

"Look at this place," Cody moans. "Broken windows, peeling paint, bashed-up porch. I could huff and puff and blow the whole house down. Looks like the wolf already blew shingles all over the grass—all over what *should* be grass, anyway."

Abby rolls her eyes. "Well, duhhhhh. That's why we're here to help."

"Yeah, Cody," Micah adds. "They told us it would be like this. What's the surprise?"

"Whatever we fix," Cody argues, "is going to fall to pieces again, anyway. If these people had any brains, they'd clean it up themselves. Why should we help them?"

Abby has an answer. "Because it's too big a job for them."

Cody plops down. "I quit. You guys are losers. I'm on a team with a bunch of nerds doing a hopeless job for people too lazy to do it themselves. This is a waste of my good talent."

☛ **Read Philippians 2:3–8. Did Jesus—the hippest person ever to hop the planet—have a big head?**

Jesus was totally God. But He didn't act like His Royal Too-High-to-Help-Out-ness. Born a baby and trained as a carpenter, He grew up and did good wherever He went—healing, feeding, making miracles, feeling people's joys and pains. And in the end, Jesus went to the cross. Even when He died for *us*—witless people who'd wasted earth—He never grumbled that His unbeatable abilities were being splattered into nothingness like a kicked-over bucket of paint.

When you're too good to hang with or help certain people—with anyone, anywhere—you're claiming a superiority God's Son scorned. Jesus didn't deny His greatness. He didn't gulp back His goodness. Instead, He used that great goodness to help people.

You don't have to bash yourself. But you can choose to count others better than yourself. To look out for more than your own interests. To serve people who need your help more than you need it yourself.

Just like Jesus.

————————

Each of you should look not only to your own interests,
but also to the interests of others. Your attitude should be the
same as that of Christ Jesus.

PHILIPPIANS 2:4–5

6

WAS THAT A BALLOON?

I t's *kabloom*, sing!" Mr. Edstrom yelled at Marsella. "*Kabloom*, sing! You hear the explosion stage right, you burst into song." The play's director fumed. "Can't make it easier. *Kabloom*, sing! Got it?" He whirled around and walked off. "Everyone—take ten!"

Marsella was aghast. She *never* got yelled at. Who did Mr. Edstrom think he was?

With opening night a week away, cast and crew were biting nails—and spitting some, too. An angry cast swarmed around Marsella. "Looks like Miss Everybody-Loves-Me froze up again," Jake mocked. "What's your problem?"

"I . . . I . . . I," Marsella stammered.

"If you hadn't been worrying about your hair holding up under the stage lights, you wouldn't have biffed your cue. You're so stuck-up. Your head is the size of a—"

Marsella started to ball.

"Poor baby," Jake jabbed, glad to make her cry. "Hey, everyone," he grinned. "Was that a balloon, or did her head just pop?"

23

☛ **Read 1 Samuel 16:1–13, where God sent the prophet Samuel to pick Israel's next king. How does God judge popularity?**

Imagine Jesse's sons strutting their stuff for God's prophet. Son Eliab thinks, *I'm the biggest.* Abinadab hums, *I'm the baddest.* Shammah's going, *I'm the brainiest.* Four more sons get scrutinized. God whispers to Samuel, "Don't be wowed by their outsides. I look at a person's insides." Samuel nixes all seven sons.

Then in walks David, the baby of the family, who'd been out walking the family sheep. "Pick him!" God shouts. "He's the one!" So Samuel pours oil on David's head—a signal of God's blessing and a warm-up for getting crowned king.

Turns out David had been in the woods working out, so he was no ugly guy. It wasn't long before he'd whup Goliath, so he was no wuss. And in time he'd run a country, so he was no dunce. But what counted to God was David's innards: David was "a man after [God's] own heart" (1 Samuel 13:14).

It's not your job to deflate others. But it *is* your job to put a pin in popularity bubbles by valuing what really counts. And you can let the air out when your own head swells. The kind of beauty, brains, and brawn that blow a head up big don't impress God. It's stuff on the inside that's worth a wow.

———

But the LORD said to Samuel, "Do not consider his
appearance or his height, for I have rejected him. The LORD
does not look at the things man looks at.
Man looks at the outward appearance,
but the LORD looks at the heart."

1 SAMUEL 16:7

TOE JAMMIN'

"Sign my yearbook?" Kathy asked sweetly. "And can I sign yours?"

Me? Huh? Scott blinked. *She wants what?* For two years Scott sat next to Kathy in math, slaving together on tough problems. But Kathy had evolved into the babe of the grade. Now she never noticed him.

"Here. Thanks!" Kathy handed back Scott's yearbook. "Gotta go. See ya!"

She just wanted all the signatures she could get, Scott thought. But she'd filled his whole back cover with stuff like "Your friendship means a lot to me" and "You're a special guy. Stay that way." Her "Call me!" and "Love, Kathy" almost made Scott pucker. Her phone number at the bottom about made him puke with excitement.

Maybe she writes that stuff in everyone's yearbook. But her phone number? Why that? A week after school quit for the summer, Scott had to find out. He called. Out fumbled "HelloitsScottyougavemeyournumberandsaidtocallhowsyoursummergoing?"

"Scott? Scott who?" she quizzed. "I don't know any Scotts."
Click.

✔ **Read Galatians 3:26–28. What's it matter that we're all "one in Christ"?**

Some people make you climb a mountain to lick dirt off their shoes. They tower over you. They treat you trashy.

True, God lets people take turns leading—as parents, teachers, bosses, police, and presidents. Some day it'll be your turn to lead, too.

Leadership is how the world holds together (Romans 13:1). But God tells powerful people not to use their God-given authority to stomp on others (Matthew 20:25–28; Ephesians 6:4).

And the fact that God grants some people positions of authority doesn't alter this huge truth about humanity: God made all people equal. Being "one in Christ Jesus" where "there is neither Jew nor Greek, slave nor free, male nor female" means that the things that might make us special—as in privileged, prideful, stuck-up, and snotty—really mean nothing. We're all equal before Him—and nothing like race, gender, status, money, looks, or power decides how much we're worth or what treatment we deserve. Christ makes us a community (people hanging together) of equality (where everyone is valuable).

So you don't have to lick anyone's shoes.

And don't make anyone tonguewash your toes.

———————

There is neither Jew nor Greek, slave nor free, male nor female,
for you are all one in Christ Jesus.

GALATIANS 3:28

26

LETTUCE HEAD

Richard stabbed the air with his pen to make his point. "I'm gonna be the next class president. Everybody knows I'm Mr. Howard's pick." Complete with bow tie and wangy hair, Richard looked like a three-quarter-size clone of Principal Howard. "I'll make a bunch of ridiculous promises." Richard was a shoo-in with all the students who thought he could actually shorten the school day. "And Lisa—she's gonna be dust in the wind."

"Don't be so sure," Lisa snarled. "By the way, you shouldn't hold your strategy sessions in the hall. And keep up that Mr. Howard look. I'll beat you for sure."

"Well, *your* posters," Richard laughed, "make you look like Marcia Brady."

"You're goin' down, Richard," Lisa stomped.

"Get ready to be buried, *Marcia*."

📝 **Read 1 Corinthians 9:24–27, where Paul tells how he fights to live for God. What's the one competition that matters most?**

Paul and the people who got his letter in Corinth knew that athletes preparing for the Isthmian Games—a huge Olympics held in Corinth—went into brutal training. Athletes did it all to win a wreath of laurel or—believe it or don't—celery.

Paul is saying, "I'm one of those guys. I'm buff. I'm tough." But Paul had picked a different fight. He competed for a different prize. What Paul sought above all was to live close to God. He fought hard to live the message he taught about Jesus.

Paul's big competition wasn't against other people. He aimed his hardest shots at himself. He was like ancient fighters who boxed with leather thongs tied to their knuckles—except he punched his *own* sin and selfishness black-and-blue to reach his goal.

Ancient athletes won prizes that wilted only a little more quickly than presidents get replaced, Miss Americas get ugly, or the rich and famous of the world get out-pizzazzed. Someone who's prettier, richer, or more popular always comes along.

But being your best for God is the one competition where winning lasts forever. Getting close to God beats hanging lettuce on your head.

Everyone who competes in the games goes into strict training.
They do it to get a crown that will not last; but we do
it to get a crown that will last forever.

1 CORINTHIANS 9:25

BELLY ITCHES

Your letter to the ultrapowerful boss at Smartypants Software ("guaranteed to make you too bright for your britches") was so brilliant he flew you to his ultraluxury compound to critique his software's ultrasecret next release.

You feel like Little Red Riding Hood meeting the Big Bad Wolf when a pack of guard dogs surround you. *My, what big teeth you have.* But the dogs heel like well-trained pups. You feed them doggie treats. They fetch. You scratch their bellies. You can't believe they're killers.

"It all depends on which side of the fence you're on," Mr. Smartypants says. "Come here and I'll show you." You walk out the compound entrance, where metal gates clang shut behind you. "Try to reach inside," he instructs. Sixteen darling puppies suddenly bare fangs at you. They bark and spring wildly into the air. "See what I mean?" he says. "Inside, they're your friends. But try to get in from the outside uninvited, and they'll maul you."

☞ **Read James 2:1–10. What makes James mad about how his readers treat people?**

Cliques are like packs of guard dogs. If you're inside their fence, they cuddle. But if you're outside, they're vicious. Depending on what they think of you, they morph from Chihuahua to chomper—or from fang to friend.

James blasted his readers for controlling who entered their group. Rich guys got good seats. Poor people got spots on the floor or shoveled out the back door. James pointed out that his readers' private little party was packed with slams, insults, and exploitation. People in the church played favorites to make the "right" friends, who were really no friends at all.

You might feel locked out of cliques. But you can't usually bust in where you're not wanted. So think hard about what you do to shut people out of *your* group. What fangs do you and your friends flash at other people? What people-proof fences do you put up?

And exactly whom are you not letting in? The point James picks on—money—is only *one* reason you might play favorites. Truth is, you can come up with a million reasons you'd show your smile and hide your snarl from people you want on your side of the fence.

My brothers, as believers in our glorious Lord Jesus
Christ, don't show favoritism.

JAMES 2:1

PASS THE OXYGEN, PLEASE

Alec heard basketballs pounding in the church gym—heard them well, in fact. Each splat and slam echoed in his under-the-staircase cave.

People were gabbing and playing hoops after youth group. Alec heard a hollered "Where's Alec? We need another player!" He smiled. *They'll never find me.*

He'd run out after midweek Bible class and ducked into his hiding spot. In a few minutes he would dart outside into the dark and his parents would pick him up. He'd get away unseen.

I can't believe all that stuff about how we're supposed to be friends. Alec thought back to what his pastor had said about "belonging to the body of Christ." *I don't think I can count on anyone here. No one cares about me. I don't feel welcome.*

He heard someone call his name again.

And then a thought shot through him: *But maybe I'm not trying.*

✒ **Read 1 Kings 19:9–19. What did God say when Elijah felt all alone?**

Life is like living underwater. Christian friends are your hose to the surface—not just for a whiff of fresh air, but for the lung-bulging oxygen you need to survive.

Elijah—a prophet, one of God's key spokespersons—counted his friends and figured he got zero. He was hated by Queen Jezebel, for instance, and hunted by her armies. He hiked for forty days and then crawled in a cave to get away.

Gently God asked Elijah why he hid. And then God heard Elijah's lonely cries. The sum of the story is this: God promised Elijah a best friend named Elisha to stand by him and carry on his mission. An even bigger bonus: Elijah could count on seven thousand other faithful-to-God Israelites who hadn't bowed to the false god Baal.

Elijah thought someone evil was standing on his air hose. Truth was, he was suffocating because he'd unhooked himself from God's people. All Elijah needed to do was to get refreshed by the friends God provided him.

There's no such thing as a scuba tank that lets you frolic through the deep waters of life all by your lonesome. You've got a lifeline, the airhose of friendship. That hose can kink, so you have to tend it carefully. But if you believe in Jesus, you're hooked up to His people. When you feel alone, ask God for Christian friends. And look around for His answer.

———

Yet I reserve seven thousand in Israel—all whose knees have not bowed down to Baal and all whose mouths have not kissed him.

1 KINGS 19:18

BACK ON THE BUS

Right after Jennifer's family moved to Asia for her dad's job, she spotted the signs on the stoplight poles: "Pedestrians should huddle together and cross the street quickly." Niffer appreciated the heads up, but she didn't have anyone to huddle with on the way to school. And where were the signs warning about cars driving on the sidewalk?

Niffer got used to dodging through the city in taxis packed so tight in the streets that they knocked mirrors. But taxis were pricey. A few students had motorscooters. But after one skidded across her toes and slid under a truck, she stayed off "murderscooters."

Niffer settled on taking the city bus to school—big, tough shell, bunches of fellow riders. Sometimes buses bullied their way down the wrong side of the road or bashed into storefronts. So she sat in the back to feel safer. After all, buses don't back into buildings.

But that didn't begin to deal with all the problems *inside* the bus. . . .

✒ **Read Isaiah 43:1–3. Who rescues you when your big, safe crowd lets you down?**

You'd like to think that traveling in a huddle protects you. But sometimes what should be a safe spot for you—a team, a youth group, a group of dependable friends—is more like a bad bus ride. You're caged with strangers. You have to watch where you sit. Whom you talk to. Who might pick your pockets. Or weird you out.

And that's still not the worst of what can happen when your herd hurts you. Sometimes the friendship bus crashes and burns.

So what happens to you then?

You have a Friend who's able to jump into the flames to rescue you. God, after all, isn't some sidewalk bystander who *might* dash to your aid. "Redeemer" means God owns the bus. And not just the bus. The people and packages and everything else onboard belong to Him (Exodus 6:6–8).

When you're riding through life and your crowd blows up on you, God is there. He's promised to rush in, pack you up in his arms, and be your friend with a fireproof blanket of love. Looking for proof? He's already rescued you from the worst crash and burn of all: sin. Jesus died to draw you close to God (Colossians 1:13–14).

You belong to God. He won't leave you alone on the bus, *especially* when the bus flames.

When you pass through the waters, I will be with you; and
when you pass through the rivers, they will not sweep over you.
When you walk through the fire, you will not be burned;
the flames will not set you ablaze.

Isaiah 43:2

DON'T DITCH YOUR DEODORANT

You were dying to see your classmates again after summer vacation. You couldn't wait to unveil your spanking-new self-assurance.

The kid at the locker next door backs away. "What happened to *you*?" he asks.

"Hiiiiiyaaaa," you breathe. He backs up further. "So you noticed? I've decided to live completely above peer pressure. I've totally stopped caring what other people think."

"Well, you look like a rat. You smell like you crawled out of a garbage pile."

"I'm happy to let you form your own opinion about me," you reassure him. "But it won't change how I act. I haven't had a shower since June. Soap, shampoo, deodorant, toothbrush, toothpaste—I threw them all away. And I've taken up public burping. Primal form of self-expression, you know. I just gotta be me. Did you know that in some cultures a hearty belch is appropriate appreciation for a well-cooked meal?"

✍ Read 2 Timothy 2:19–22. What's good about peer pressure?

Peer fear. Teachers lecture you about it. Parents shield you from it. And anti-drug, anti-thug, anti-smoking, anti-drinking TV commercials try to scare you out of it. Peer fear is when you let the expectations of others egg you on. It's when you try so hard to please other people that you go where you know you shouldn't. But not all *peer pressure* is *beer pressure*—a big push to swill alcohol, torch your brain on drugs, or mouth off to your parents.

Everybody needs *good* peer pressure—a healthy dread of what other people think. Good peer pressure is the deodorant of life. It stops life's little stinks.

Still, there's an even better peer pressure, a kind that launches you way past a belch-free life-style. The *best* peer pressure helps you choose God and His good ways.

In big houses, Paul says, there are both cheap dishes and china. When you make pleasing God the most important thing in life, you're choosing to be china. God will use you to do great things.

Here's the catch: You won't become more than a paper plate all on your own. You ditch evil best—and chase God the hardest—when you hang with peers who want to follow God. You need their *best* pressure to push and pull you to God's greatest stuff.

———

Flee the evil desires of youth, and pursue righteousness, faith,
love and peace, along with those who call on the
Lord out of a pure heart.

2 TIMOTHY 2:22

13

HE'S A HUMAN HOCKEY PUCK

Ching-thwipp. Another shot off the post and into the net behind Justin.

"Sorry, guys," Justin apologized—again.

Justin grew up on an iceless planet. When he settled in a different place, he found his new friends had feet built with blades instead of toes. Well, more or less. Slotting Justin in the goal kept him out of their way, but even tiny shuffle steps back and forth in the net sent Justin skidding on the ice like a human hockey puck.

Most days no one cared. But this time his friends got ornery. Justin came home with a cut-up lip and a blood-soaked jacket. Not that anyone had slugged him. He got bashed up when they shoved him and he slammed onto the ice.

"Justin, what are you trying to prove?" his older sister pleaded. "You're good at English. You're pretty great at chess. You thrash those guys at basketball and—"

"But nobody cares about any of that stuff," Justin moaned. "All they know is that I can't play hockey."

☞ **Read Romans 12:3–8. What good does it do to decide what makes you great?**

You can go back to back with your friends to see who's taller. You can flex your biceps to see who's bigger. And you can get out a measuring tape to put a precise number on who-thrashes-whom. But the most accurate measurement of who you really are—no more, no less—is figuring out what good gifts God has built inside you.

God made you good at something. You may recognize yourself in the list of "spiritual gifts" Paul put here (or in his lists in 1 Corinthians 12:7–10 and Ephesians 4:11–12). You may be the total math tutor. Or someone whose shoulder is soaked with the tears of hurting friends. You may be the tightest writer your classmates have ever read. Or you may be a rock-steady influence on one close friend. Celebrate that!

You may still be figuring out what makes you unique. That's okay.

You can't quit everything you're no good at. No one gets out of serving and supporting others. No one gets out of school. But it's okay to boldly put to use your unique talents. What you're good at may not make you popular. But what you're good at is what makes you good for this world (1 Corinthians 12:7; Ephesians 2:10).

———

We have different gifts, according to
the grace given us.

ROMANS 12:6

BETTER
THAN BUFF

Try it again, Bekka. Like this." Shawna stepped into the blocks. At the sound of an imaginary starting gun, Shawna exploded. She screamed past Bekka and soared over three hurdles before jogging back.

"I can't do that!" Bekka moaned. "You look like a gazelle or something."

"A gazelle? Gazelles smell," Shawna sassed back. "But thanks. By the way, you do great, too."

"By the way, I do *not*." Bekka got quiet. "Shawna, that's why I'm going to tell coach you should take my spot as team captain. You're way better than I am. You're way better than the whole state. You never put anyone down, you listen to everyone, and you're great at helping people. Before you came over here, I was so frustrated I was ready to wrap a hurdle around someone's head."

"I'm glad I could help," Shawna said, "because I like to help people. But it's God who makes me run fast. You're making too big a deal of *me*."

41

☞ Read Jeremiah 9:23–24. What does God say is the one thing worth bragging about?

You invite a new friend to your house. You'd be totally mannerless if: a) you dragged her in the door and over the dog to see your best-ever report card—the one your mom blew up to cover the whole front of the fridge; b) you wildly arm-wrestled her until your superior musculature ripped her rotator cuff; c) you beat her mercilessly on your billion-bit Nintendo system; or, actually, d) all of the above.

Brainiacs are bright. Body builders are buff. Millionaires are marvy. It's fun to ace the test, win the race, get the prize. But all our knowledge, might, and money are small things compared to the greatness of knowing God.

He's the one worth bragging about.

When you feel like bursting out in a song of praise, don't screech about yourself. Say stuff about God, who is absolutely kind, fair, and right. His faithfulness clears hurdles higher than the sky. His bright, shining glory races around the earth (Psalm 108:3–5). You may be a big deal, but God is way biggest.

———————

"Let him who boasts boast about this: that he understands and knows me, that I am the LORD, who exercises kindness, justice and righteousness on earth, for in these I delight," declares the LORD.

JEREMIAH 9:24

SLICK
OR SLOB

I can't believe Tadd pays attention to them, Jake fumed. *They're wrecking everything.*

Jake stared at his youth pastor as he talked to some of the newbies in his church youth group. They goofed off. Some stunk of smoke. And last summer when Tadd took most of the group to sing in churches in South Dakota, Jake went on a mission trip to South America. *They got in a street brawl,* Jake recalled smugly. *I was a missionary.*

A little later Tadd rapped on Jake's head—and it was like he'd read Jake's mind. "They aren't going to get fixed all at once, you know. God's working on them. Jake, think about it. You used to be mouthy. Did you shut up right away—even when you got serious about following God?"

Jake remembered it took him a while to break a bunch of bad habits.

"Jake, most of these kids have gotten kicked around bad. Think about ways to help them up, not to push them down."

☛ **Read Galatians 6:1–5. What should you think when you can do something well that others can't?**

You might be embarrassed when report cards go home. You might hide from footballs or figure skates. You might cringe when people eye your less-than-lovable clothes. But sooner or later in life you'll land on something where you're slick—and most everyone else is a slob.

Take your faith, for example. If you pay half a brain's worth of attention in Sunday school, you may think you're a saint. Truth is, you are—but not because of anything *you* did. Because of Christ's death for you, you're truly a saint (Colossians 1:12). Because of His life in you, you've got gifts to help you change the world (1 Peter 4:10). And truth is, apart from God we're all spiritual slobs. Whatever good things we possess, God gave us (1 Corinthians 4:7). And we're to use our spiritual strength to hoist people out of sin.

That truth that God has given us everything good fits all of life. You can always find someone badder—and feel better. You can always find someone better—and feel badder. What matters is what's up with you. Are you doing your best? If you're doing well, who got you there? And how are you using your strengths to help others?

When you're doing better than others, thank God for how He's helped you. And figure out who you can help, too.

Each one should test his own actions. Then he can take pride in himself, without comparing himself to somebody else. . . .

GALATIANS 6:4–5

CANNIBAL
LUNCH

You thought they were your friends, but now they're fixin' to have *filet of you*. They've got you hog-tied and hanging over a boiling cauldron.

You beg them to slow down. You try to buy time. All you want is a chance to wiggle around—and run away. But there's no chance of escape.

You try to remind them of all the times *they* said or did something you didn't like—and how you let them off the hook.

You can't convince them to converse.

They dip in your toe so you can feel the burn.

Then they get a hotter idea.

They don't even bother to cook you.

They eat you raw.

📝 **Read 1 Peter 4:12–19. What do you do when people pick on you?**

Kids who bug you come and go. And come again. It's a fact of life: When one drifts away, another one just as annoying or bruising drifts right in. The fact that people will pester you is permanent (John 16:33). Some folks may even hate you (1 John 3:13). And sometimes even best friends hang you over a hot pot (Psalm 41:9).

Peter separates the pain of those cannibal lunches—the peer-eat-peer of daily life—from an even bigger, tougher-to-endure kind of suffering.

Peter's saying this: When you get boiled for stuff like putting a fork in other people—murder—or putting your nose in other people's stuff—meddling—you can't blame your suffering on anyone but yourself. God won't let you wiggle free just because you belong to Him.

But when you catch wrong for doing right—no boiling deserved—you're suffering for a bigger reason. You're suffering for Jesus.

That's when you'd really like God to help you off the hook. But it's also when God puts a huge choice to you: Will you turn tough, hate God, and try to boil those who boil you? Or will you keep doing good God's way?

So then, those who suffer according to God's will should
commit themselves to their faithful Creator
and continue to do good.

1 PETER 4:19

LEFTOVER TUNABUDDY HOTDISH

Leftover tuna hotdish stared at Megan from the refrigerator shelf—a heaping bowl of over-boiled noodles and oily tuna mixed in with a mound of mushy peas. *Blechhhhh. Not a chance, tunabuddy.* Nothing against her mom's cooking—and she didn't want to be ungrateful for food—but a dish that was worth her wolfing down wouldn't be camping in megaquantities in the fridge.

Megan dug behind the tuna, but the unidentifiable food farther back had sprouted legs and was plotting its escape. So Megan reached for stuff to make her trusty pickle and peanut butter sandwich. But the kitchen was bare of bread.

With her parents out at a movie and her older brother out with friends, Megan threw herself a pity party. *Just me, TV, and a hearty helping of tuna hotdish*, Megan pouted. She stabbed the hotdish with a fork. *This stuff's just like me. I'm a leftover.*

☛ Read Psalm 73:21–28. How do you cope when life leaves you all alone?

Some days you feel like you've been tossed over a cliff. You're clinging to a twig like an over-the-edge cartoon character. You're alone. You're hurting. You scream for help. You wonder if a rescue squad will ever arrive.

Even though you're stabbed with fear, you're also smart. You won't be fooled by a make-believe rope that can't do you any good. You know that wishing won't make a rope magically appear.

When a real rope flings down from above, you recognize it. You cling to it. You loop it around your waist and tie it tight.

When you holler for God, you're not calling into nothingness. You're asking for real help.

God exists. He's no fairy-tale wish, no magic rope. God promises to meet your needs (Philippians 4:19). He promises—in His perfect way, in His perfect time—to come to your rescue (Psalm 72:12–14). And most of all, He promises to be with you no matter what (Hebrews 13:5).

When you're lonely, grab hold of God. He's all you need. He's real help for real life.

———————

My flesh and my heart may fail, but God is the strength
of my heart and my portion forever. . . .
It is good to be near God.

PSALM 73:26–28

18

RIP YOUR BUNS OFF

The name "Mr. Headcrusher" should have been clue *numero uno*. But the guy who emerged in a splash of fireworks as the night's next wrestler looked scary even from your seventy-eighth row seat.

The voice of the master of ceremonies reverbs through the arena. "The next match-*atch-atch*," he roars, "involves audience-*ence-ence* participation-*tion-tion*."

You wonder what audience member would be fool enough to participate in the ring with that thing. But *you* are about to be the fool. The crowd chants, "YOU! YOU! YOU!" You're bodypassed to the front. You're heaved into the ring.

"I'm going to tear you to pieces," Mr. Headcrusher growls as he circles you. "And when I'm done, kid, I'm gonna rip your buns off and make 'em into earmuffs."

📖 **Read Matthew 10:28–31. Who's the most fearsome guy in the universe?**

Right before the chunk of Bible you just read, Jesus told His disciples what to expect when they went out to talk about Him. Some folks would welcome them warmly. Others would try to waste them.

The world can be a pressure-filled place when you follow Jesus. You *plus* a crowd *plus* the ring of life *equals* a crushing experience.

Yet if the world is tough, God's even tougher. If you think peers can powerbomb you, wait until you see what God can do to His enemies. If you're not on God's side, you've picked a reserved seat in a hideous place where His Son never shines.

But God's goal isn't to shred you. While these are some of the Bible's most straight-talking words (verse 28), they're tag-teamed with some of its most tender (verses 29–31). God knows the flight plan of every sparrow on earth—those tiny speckled birds that wing outside your window. They sold in ancient markets for next to nothing—two for a penny. But God watches over you infinitely more closely. He knows the smallest details of who you are. He cares about the frailest parts of *you*.

That's a good reminder to stick on the right side.

———

Do not be afraid of those who kill the body but cannot kill the soul. Rather, be afraid of the One who can destroy both soul and body in hell.

MATTHEW 10:28

19

IF YOU'RE HAPPY AND YOU KNOW IT

Keith shivered in a sweat shirt, jeans, and blanket. After working on an African mission trip in hundred-degree-plus heat for a whole summer, he felt frozen.

His friends sat comfortably in the cool evening air. They thought he was crazy.

Keith quietly told how he had helped build a house at an orphanage, how he'd gotten to know the orphans, and how God now led his life.

Talking about spiritual stuff came easy. If Keith's body had been toasted in the heat, his spiritual brainage had gotten lit on fire. Keith burned to know Jesus. And obey Him. He'd figured out that Jesus wanted to be his one-of-a-kind friend.

His friends sat comfortably in their spiritual coolness. They thought he was loony.

The next day his best friend passed him a letter a bunch of people had signed. "We think you should stop talking about Jesus. We don't want to hear about that."

✒ Read Matthew 10:32–33. Why admit that you know Jesus?

Some people think Christians are like telephone salespeople. They call during dinner. They won't quit grabbing your ear until your food goes cold. They sell stuff you don't want—and at rip-off prices. If you're smart, you hang up before they start.

God isn't into obnoxious words of faith. You don't have to wear a sign, pin, bracelet, or T-shirt—or stick a fish onto the tail end of your family roadster. But you do need to be okay with being known as someone who belongs to God.

Peter says that once you know God, you need to have some simple words ready: "Give an answer to everyone who asks you to give the reason for the hope that you have." But those words should also be kind: "Do this with gentleness and respect" (1 Peter 3:15).

Sometimes, though, even close followers of God quake when people put down their faith. Once upon a time, big Peter crumbled when a little servant asked if he knew Jesus (Luke 22:55–62). Even Paul went to Jerusalem to meet with church leaders out of fear he had missed the whole point of his faith (Galatians 2:1–2). But those guys knew God. They grew strong. They got bold.

You know God. You belong to Someone great. Don't be afraid to say it, even when others think you're crazy.

"Whoever acknowledges me before men, I will also acknowledge him before my Father in heaven."

MATTHEW 10:32

WOOF!
WOOF!

S he's still a dog," Melissa laughed. "But at least we taught her to heel. *Woof! Woof!*"

Melissa and her summer camp cabinmates guffed huge guffaws. Jane was their charity case—their project for the week to "woof proof." They'd shown her how to shave her legs. They'd talked her into letting them do her hair. They'd shoveled on makeup to smooth her skin. They'd each donated a shirt or a pair of shorts. And they coached her in what to say for maximum boy appeal. By the time they got done with Jane, she looked like a big-haired poodle at a poochie beauty contest.

Suddenly Jane stood in the cabin door.

She'd shaken out the new 'do and wiped off all the makeup. She wore her own clothes. And she looked like the cozy old Jane. "I appreciate what you did," she stammered. "But I liked myself the way I was. I'm not anything fancy, but I'm me."

✒ **Read Psalm 139:1–16. Who likes you no matter what other people think?**

You're geek of the week, getting picked on for temporary flaws. You dropped the ball, tanked the test, inserted your foot in your mouth and chewed vigorously.

Or you feel like the lice of life, enduring teasing about things that might never go away. If you're big like a truck, they say you beep when you back up. If you're bony like boards sticking out the rear end of a car, they tell you to tie a yellow flag to your backside.

Name something that makes you unique and people have probably poked fun at it.

God knows you inside and out. After all, He made you inside and out. And He loves what He sees. All the things that make you *you*—how you think and feel and look and act—He can't get enough of those.

God sometimes works to change you—to rid your life of sin and to keep you from hurling into hurt (Psalm 32:1–11). But He's always chasing you to strengthen and support you. Ponder this: You'd go berserk looking for a misplaced five-dollar bill. You'd ditch school for a day to look for a lost fifty. You'd spend your life tracking down a trillion. God pursues you like you're a trillion trillions.

You're no *bow-wow-woof-woof*. A little wacky, maybe. Your own person, definitely. And in His eyes, wonderful, undoubtedly.

———

I praise you because I am fearfully and wonderfully
made; your works are wonderful,
I know that full well.

PSALM 139:14

21

THE WINNINGEST COACH IN THE WORLD

The mother of the pitcher screams from the stands: "Come on! Blow it right by!"

The catcher tries his hardest to tip your brain off balance: "Hey, *battah battah battah*, suh-wing, *battah battah battah*."

The pitcher throws you a tough one. The ball seems to laugh: "I'm a sizzling loop-de-doop-knuckle-fisted-sidearm curve."

And some guy yells from behind the backstop, mere feet from you. His words rattle in your helmet: "Look at me when I'm talking to you!"

You refuse to be distracted. You glance at your bench. Your coach watches you calmly. Nods encouragement. Claps hands to tell you, "Get going. Eyes on the ball."

You hear the backstop guy again: "I said *look at me when I'm talking to you!*" This time you spin in your spikes to look. He stares you straight in the eyes.

Huh? Who's he? And why's he yelling at me?

📖 **Read Acts 4:13–21. What did Peter and John say when religious leaders tried to keep them from talking about Jesus?**

If a backstop stranger says your stance is too wide or you need to square-up to the plate, he's hollering good advice probably worth taking. But if he says you should swing blindfolded or slide into home plate on your face, he's clearly not rooting for you.

But there's a bigger point. When you play ball, you answer to *one* voice: your coach. Bystanders aren't your boss. The waterboy can't signal you to steal second. Your best friend can't tell you to swing for a home run if your coach calls a bunt.

By God's power Peter and John had just healed a man who couldn't walk (Acts 3:1–10). They were giving credit to Jesus, and the religious leaders who had opposed Jesus wanted Peter and John to tape their mouths shut. That clearly contradicted God's command to speak up about faith (Acts 1:8), and God's guys had one response: "We've got *one* coach. We obey *His* voice" (see both Acts 4:19 and 5:29).

Jesus is the clear, calm voice calling to you above the roar of the crowd.

You win when you listen to Him.

But Peter and John replied, "Judge for yourselves
whether it is right in God's sight
to obey you rather than God."

Acts 4:19

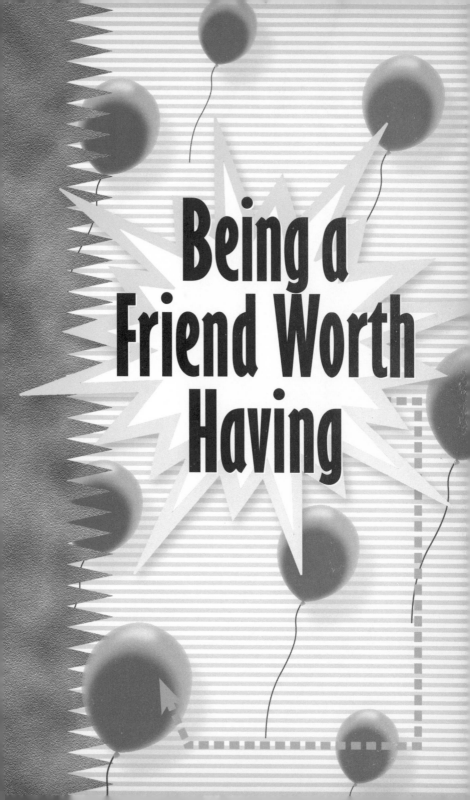

Being a Friend Worth Having

22

SHOPPING AT THE CAR SHOW

You've never seen such a sea of sculpted metal and glass. When your parents dart left into minivan and family sedan land, you dodge right in search of monster sports-utility vehicles and rocket-cockpit sports cars.

Suddenly in front of you is your all-time favorite auto. Unoccupied.

All mine—for a minute, you think. You settle into the seat, play with the mirrors, land your head on the headrest. You wrap your hands around the leather wheel, close your eyes, and dream about scooting a hundred miles an hour down a dirt road.

Wake me up when I've got my license.

This is better than any racing game at the arcade.

This is the real thing.

Well, only sort of. You can't test-drive a car at an auto show.

✒ **Read Psalm 34:8–22. What good does it do you to follow God?**

Life is no car show. It's a speedway. A road rally. A demolition derby.

Good news: God doesn't just look hot on the show floor. He tests best in the real race of life. "Check me out," He says. "Take me for a spin. See how I do." Drive with Him once, and you'll never settle for anything less than His quality closeness and care—and His pedal-to-the-floor, hang-tight-to-your-seat blessings.

And following God has what car salesfolk call "the intangible benefits of ownership." Believe it or don't, hanging with a zoomy Lord as leader of your life can bring you friendship when you least expect it—and for deeper reasons than people flock to a beautiful car.

Here's why: Whenever you get on the path of following God, you find others on the same path (Psalm 119:63). As you do His will, you deepen friendships and help others (Ecclesiastes 4:10). You find still more friends as you share God's friendship (Matthew 11:19). But most of all, getting soaked in God's love strengthens you to spread His care (1 John 4:19).

God is worth following. If you let Him, He makes you into a person who'd make a great friend. After all, it's like your mom says: If you want friends, you have to be a friend worth having.

———

Taste and see that the LORD is good; blessed is the
man who takes refuge in him.

PSALM 34:8

23

I'VE HAD ENOUGH

Everyone at school lives in big houses," Brett yelled at his dad. "None of them wear stupid clothes like mine. They won't hang around with people like me." Brett wanted a spending spree. *Now.*

A few days later Brett piled into the car with his dad. When Brett noticed they were taking a long detour on the way to the mall, his dad waved off his questions.

"Brett," his dad finally said, "before we go shopping, I want you to see something. Not so you feel guilty, but so you know what we've got." They stopped in front of a run-down house, one hardly bigger than Brett's friends' playhouses. A guy sat on the front stoop cleaning a handgun. Garages were sprayed with gang graffiti.

"I know we don't have a huge house," Brett's dad said, "but we have a lot to thank God for." Brett's dad pointed at the tiny place. "I haven't been by here since you were little. This is where your grandpa and grandma lived when I was born."

✒ **Read Matthew 5:3. How can you be wildly happy, no matter what?**

Matthew 5:3–11 contains what Bible buffs call the "Beatitudes" (say it like "be" plus "attitudes"). In some Bibles these bites of truth start with the word "Blessed," as in *"Blessed* are the poor in spirit." But it's just as correct to say "Happy," like other Bibles do, as in *"Happy* are the poor in spirit." If being blessed sounds gaggy to you, being happy probably sounds a whopper more appetizing.

So listen up as we work through these wild words of Jesus. They're keys to the kind of person God wants you to be, and they're ways He frees you to be a great friend.

In the verse you just read, Jesus is saying more than "Have an attitude of gratitude," though that's crucial (1 Timothy 6:17).

His point is this: When you think you've got nothing, you've got everything you need. You might feel short on friends. You might be truly penniless. Either way, you've got God. People who are poor in spirit—or just plain poor (Luke 6:20)—possess the kingdom of heaven.

Having a gargantuan house or a stunning wardrobe won't make your life perfect. When all you hold in your hands is God, you've got the stuff that really counts.

Blessed are the poor in spirit, for theirs is the
kingdom of heaven.

Matthew 5:3

OKAY
TO HURT

Britney sat against the back wall of the church. She couldn't drag herself to the front, close to her best friend's open casket. Lakeesha was dead, and now Britney was dying on the inside. People said Lakeesha was in heaven. All Britney knew was that she wasn't here with her anymore.

What bugged Britney most was that hardly anyone talked about Lakeesha. The adults chitchatted about the weather and how tough it was to be a kid these days. The kids gabbed about school and mean teachers and stupid homework. It was like Lakeesha never existed. Just like how her locker was already cleaned out.

Britney's insides were screaming to talk about *all* of it. No one else wanted to talk about *any* of it. When it came to pain, her crowd had two rules: 1) guys aren't supposed to cry, and 2) girls are supposed to get over it.

Britney's mom suggested she tell God how bad she was hurting.

"God?" Britney said. "Why God? He doesn't have a clue what I'm feeling."

☛ Read Matthew 5:4. What good is God when you're hurting?

You're probably good at faking tough. You learned to be tough when you tipped off your bike and ripped up your leg and forced yourself to stop crying. You got to practice toughness when you got a good scab going and someone came by and kicked your shin.

God doesn't make you fake toughness. When you cry to Him, He comforts you. When you wail to Him, you're talking to someone who's always listening. He's your always-present help in trouble (Psalm 46:1).

God understands loss. He's watched His coolest creation—human beings—ditch friendship with Him and devour each other. He witnessed the death of His Son, Jesus, for all the evil of the world.

God has hurt figured out.

There's more news: While God won't bash your sadness, He also won't let you wallow in it. He heals you, then lets you help heal others. Whenever God comforts you, you can pass that care on (2 Corinthians 1:3–4).

Blessed are those who mourn,
for they will be comforted.

Matthew 5:4

25

MOVE IT OR LOSE IT, PUS-BRAIN

Tyler knew to step aside, just like he was shrewd enough to get out of the path of a raging steamroller.

All Tyler wanted was to get to his assigned assembly seat in the auditorium's nosebleeds. But as he trudged upward, he saw "the Mob"—the six most popular guys in middle school, plus their girls—rushing up from below, ready to run him over. Smart boy: Tyler scampered out of the aisle and into a row of seats to let them pass. But the Mob stopped at the same spot.

"Hey, pus-brain," they steamed at Tyler. "Those are our seats."

That they were. And the Mob wasn't moving. So Tyler took the only way out—the long way down the other end of the row. Half the auditorium watched him bumble over twenty other yelping bodies already in their seats.

He lived—but he'd had to lick ground.

☑ **Read Matthew 5:5. What's it mean to be meek?**

You can't take it personally when people pick on you. Mean people are like a mosquito pack that buzzes away tanked up on your blood. You may feel like a particularly plump, juicy target. Truth is, they suck blood any place they can get it.

Sometimes you can stand up for your rights by speaking truth (Ephesians 4:15), relying on the authorities God put in place to make things right (Romans 13:1–5), or running for help when you can't solve a problem yourself (Matthew 18:15–17).

But other times there's no escape. You'll get the stuffing beat out of you. You'll get stomped on your way to the cheap seats. Some days you'll get steamrollered. Other days you'll get sucked dry.

Meekness ain't weakness. Meekness is gentle, self-controlled strength. Meekness means being something better than the bullies who beat up the world. God is on the side of the gentle, and Jesus tells us who *won't* win the ultimate popularity and power contest—the proud, strong, aggressive, harsh, and tyrannical who suck life from others.

Inheriting the earth means God gives a prize—someday, some way—for every pint of blood you give up. So it's clear who the real losers are.

Blessed are the meek, for they will inherit the earth.

MATTHEW 5:5

26

MORE
THAN A
MARK MCGWIRE
CARD

tefan and his friends crowded into the best baseball card store in town—an overgrown newsstand that sold everything from bubble gum to baseball cards, to magazines and papers from all over the world.

But his buddies were looking for more than a Mark McGwire card.

"Don't think so hard, Stefan," they told him. "Just take it."

"It" was a skin magazine to be bought with a five-finger discount.

It wasn't that Stefan was an uncurious, hormone-free kind of guy. But he could think of a few fatal reasons to say no: 1) getting shot for shoplifting; 2) getting grilled by his parents for looking at porn; 3) the pledge he'd made to stay sexually pure—and porn-free was part of that; and 4) how awful he felt when he deliberately did something wrong.

Four strikes—his friends were out. Stefan walked away. "If you want it," he told them, "*you* steal it. See ya. I'm going home."

✍ **Read Matthew 5:6. Are you a fool to play by the rules?**

You want to do what's right. But lots of times cheaters grab better grades. Shoplifters score more stuff. Devious kids do wrong and then lie to get out of punishment. They all grab what they want for themselves—and they almost always get to keep it. You feel deprived.

God will smoke people who don't ditch sin (Revelation 21:8). But that's another topic.

And besides, what's that end-of-the-world truth do for you? Right now, you might still be spectator to evil's spectacular success.

One great thing about good: If you do right, you have nothing to fear (Romans 13:3). That beats being afraid of getting in trouble.

But another great thing: When you hunger for God and His ways, God fills you up so you can be wildly happy doing what's best. When you really want righteousness—right attitudes and actions, inside and out—He remakes you to want to be good not only for your own sake but also for the world around you to work right.

And whenever you want God's right thing in God's right time, He'll give it to you.

———

Blessed are those who hunger and thirst for righteousness, for they will be filled.

MATTHEW 5:6

ONE GOOD REASON

In the dirt. *Ball one.*

Into the bleachers. *Ball two.*

Monica launches the softball toward home plate, and it barely brushes by the batter's back. *Ball three.* Bekah—the batter—tosses back a threat: "One more pitch like that, girl, and I'll push that ball in one of your ears and make a new hole to pull it out."

Monica again sends the ball toward home plate—but this time it bonks Bekah's head. *Ball four.*

In an instant Bekah is at the mound, and with her one swift shove Monica is flat on the ground, Bekah pinning her down, arm cocked to punch.

"Give me one good reason why I shouldn't hit you."

Monica, unfortunately, isn't a fast thinker.

✔ Read Matthew 5:7. Why be merciful?

Jesus told a story about a servant who owed his master a monstrous stash of cash. When the servant heard that he, his wife, and

69

children were to be jailed for the debt, he begged for mercy. In response, the master forgave the servant's debt and let him go. One day, though, the servant bumped into a man who owed the servant a relatively tiny amount of money. When that man couldn't cough it up, the servant had him tossed in prison. The master, on hearing this, understandably went berserk. He tossed his servant in prison after all.

Big point: "This," Jesus said, "is how my heavenly Father will treat each of you unless you forgive your brother from your heart" (Matthew 18:35).

You—and I—and everyone else on the planet—have done wrong. Sinned. Piled up a big, unpaybackable bill. Jesus, though, paid the penalty—death—that God decreed for your debt of sin (Romans 6:23). And forgiveness of your sin is free for the asking. John wrote, "If we confess our sins, he is faithful and just and will forgive us our sins" (1 John 1:9).

That's God's Good News. But it's silly to say you believe in your need and have said "yes!" to God's mercy if you can't show mercy to others. Fighting back with fists or fingernails or foul mouths means you haven't figured out what God has done for you.

You'll get back what you dish out.

Blessed are the merciful,
for they will be shown mercy.

MATTHEW 5:7

28

DETHRONE THE SLEAZE QUEENS

Heather had heard about "the Sleaze Queens" long before she graduated into her new school. And she spotted Becki and Bobbi her first day at the place.

Becki and Bobbi were twins who lived up to their wicked nick-name. They had a reputation for being, um, sleazy—and from high atop their throne of popularity, they managed to control the entire social scene of Woodlake Middle School.

They had decreed that any girl without a boyfriend was hence-forth and forevermore a loser. Never mind that the boys knew more about the finer points of making armpit noises than they did treating girls fine. Or that no girl or guy needs to get locked up in a relationship that sooner or later leads nowhere good.

Heather was—by the Sleaze Queens' quite official rules of the school—a loser.

And know what? Knowing she was doing the right thing didn't automatically make her feel better.

☛ Read Matthew 5:8. What does purity look like in real life?

You ache when you're left out for making right choices. If purity were just about rules, you'd have reason to feel rotten. But it's better than that.

Yep, purity is about *performance—how you act*. It's about obedience and conforming to God's commands. But conforming isn't contorting—twisting yourself into a pretzel just because someone makes you.

Purity is also about *purpose—how you think and feel*. Jesus said that real purity starts with the heart (Matt 5:21–22, 27–28). Not whomping an enemy is stupendous—but not if you're still stuffed full of hatred. Sweet sixteen and never been kissed sure beats sweet sixteen and never been missed—but not if you still champ at the get-a-boyfriend-or-girlfriend bit. Obeying your parents is right on track—but you've derailed if you still steam on the inside.

Get this: Purity is most of all about a *person—how you live close to Jesus*. It's no mystery. Purity isn't misery. Jesus said that anyone who serves Him follows Him (John 12:26). Real purity wants right stuff and sticks close to Jesus' side. It's true: The pure in heart see God.

And having Jesus close by beats holding hands with an armpit-blasting boyfriend.

Blessed are the pure in heart, for they will see God.

MATTHEW 5:8

TRUE PEACE

Mayerly Sanchez remembers a close friend, Milton, buried two years before. "The day before he died," whispers Mayerly, "we had been playing soccer in the street." Stabbed in a gang fight in a suburb of Bogota, Colombia, Milton was one of thirty thousand people who died violently in his country that year.

At his funeral, Mayerly vowed to work for peace.

Mayerly now co-leads a national peace movement of almost three million kids. Their work has influenced more than ten million Colombians to vote "yes" to a Citizen's Mandate for Peace that highlights love, acceptance, forgiveness, and work.

She discusses legislation with Colombian congressmen and speaks to conferences at leading universities.

She's been nominated for a Nobel Peace Prize.

She's fourteen.

☞ Read Matthew 5:9. How can you make peace in a world at war?

Statistically, you can count on 98.6 percent of the contestants in any beauty pageant to stroll the stage and state that their deepest wish in life is world peace. (Right after acquiring big hair, mondo manicured nails, and a beachside condo like Barbie's.)

They're blowing smoke to try to win a tinsel crown. Mayerly, though, does *real* stuff to try to stop the killing in a country with a murder rate fifteen times that of the United States.

To Mayerly, being a peacemaker is part of daily life. "We heard a lot about peace in the media," one fifteen-year-old Colombian said. "But Mayerly taught us that peace needs to be practiced. If we see two of our friends fighting, we need to intervene and try to motivate them to get along."

Mayerly's peacemaking didn't start with halting drug lords and their hired thugs. It began with how she acts at home and with friends.

Your peacemaking won't start with stomping out crime in the central city—though it can lead there. It begins with how you treat your bratty siblings and the pest who sits behind you in science.

You might not win a Nobel Prize. But when you spread peace among your ranting friends and raving family and raging enemies, you show them you belong to the Prince of Peace (Isaiah 9:6–7).

———————

Blessed are the peacemakers,
for they will be called sons of God.

MATTHEW 5:9

STAND DOWNWIND

As soon as they hit seventh grade, Brock and his friends started having weekly weekend parties. Back then the boys hid the dance CDs in the microwave so the girls couldn't find them. By eighth grade couples were tongue-wrestling on the couch. By ninth grade kids were sipping wine coolers and belching beers.

Brock told himself that other parties and places were a lot worse. Yet he had a queasy certainty he should have quit the parties a *looooong* time ago. But the kids who did the parties were his best friends. His only friends. All of his friends, actually.

And they told Brock the stuff they did was no big deal. When he said it was, they bagged him. And before he could stop going to the parties, they stopped inviting him.

> **Read Matthew 5:10–12. What's it mean to be "persecuted for righteousness"?**

You're in a situation and you're feeling weird. You wonder if it's you—or if it's Jesus.

75

Get it straight: You can't blame all your own random weirdnesses on God.

But you know that. When people look at you funny, you look at yourself to see if it's something you can fix. You do a deodorant check. You flip a TicTac. You stand downwind when you chat. You do your best to act normal—within God's limits, of course.

And you still wind up thinking, *Hmm . . . I don't fit here.*

And you ponder, *Hmm . . . this is about right and wrong.*

And you conclude, *Hmm . . . I belong to Jesus—and if I decided to disobey Him, this problem would go away.*

Then it's about Jesus.

People all over the planet are persecuted—sometimes solely for their beliefs, sometimes for a nasty knot of ethnic and economic and spiritual issues. You might or might not ever be persecuted like that. You're not likely to be picked on like people in Christian movies who don't bow to the Beast and get guillotined. Yet you'll surely catch some "all kinds of evil against you." And a lot of times persecution for making the right choice means you get ignored with a fury. People don't mistreat you. They don't beat you. They just forget you.

Massive is your reward.

———————

Blessed are those who are persecuted because of righteousness, for theirs is the kingdom of heaven . . . great is your reward.

MATTHEW 5:10, 12

DOING
THE 'TUDES

Kaitlin and Josh glared at their youth pastor. They hadn't liked their assignment very much—to go ask a non-Christian what she or he thinks of Christians.

"I asked Mr. Riley whether he saw anything in me that made him want to be a Christian," Josh reported. "He said he didn't buy what I was selling. He said I blow up all the time. He pretty much called me a hypocrite."

"And I talked to Miss Fernandez, my Spanish teacher," Kaitlin said. "My question asked, 'How are Christians different from other people?' She said 'Can I be blunt? Christians aren't different—they're *weird*.'"

Read Matthew 5:13–16. Why would you want to follow Jesus' words?

You want to do right. But not if it's hopelessly hard. Not just "because God said so." So why listen to what you might think are wacky, unworkable words in the Beatitudes? Why "do the 'tudes"?

Reason #1: *Doing the 'tudes makes you happy.* Okay, maybe a different kind of happy than an amusement park whizzy-woosy-with-glee. But people who live by the words Jesus uttered stick close to God and run smack into His blessings.

Reason #2: *Doing the 'tudes makes you a person who makes a splash for good in a nasty world.* You're spice—tasty flavor. You're light—a beam on God's right way.

Reason #3: *Doing the 'tudes shows off God's power.* He's making you spiritually hungry, honest about pain, gentle, merciful, pure, peaceful, and patient in persecution. Powerful stuff—and powerfully attractive, whether or not people realize it right away.

Non-Christians don't need our bumper stickers or T-shirts—they're looking for God's good stuff inside us. How we vote won't transmogrify the world—though voting is swell. We're not distinguished by our health or wealth—in fact, we search for better riches. And we don't rub our goodness in people's faces—that isn't what Jesus meant by being "a city set on a hill." (Check out what He says a few verses later in Matthew 6:1–6.)

If you want to be happy, do good, make friends, and show off God, Jesus gave you the list of the 'tudes He's building in you.

You are the salt of the earth. . . . You are the light of the world. A city on a hill cannot be hidden. . . . Let your light shine before men, that they may see your good deeds and praise your Father in heaven.

MATTHEW 5:13, 14, 16

Lettin' God Into Your Life

*S*PIRITUAL
BELLY BUTTON*S*

*S*HWOOP! FINGAFINGAFINGA! SPRANKkank*kank!*

Stunned, you stare at a sewer lid that's blown off the street, caught air like a Frisbee, and landed at your feet.

But you only look at the lid for a second. Intergalactic aliens dead ahead!

You'd been strutting down your home street when a couple real sewer-cloggers blocked your path. Suddenly thankful for all the stranger-danger and self-defense stuff you'd gotten in school, you punt the aliens back to where they came from, thereby preserving life as we know it on planet earth.

Not unexpectedly, you're recruited into the government's ultrasecret alien-fighting corps. You get the standard issue dark suit and shades. Your identity is erased. You're invisible. You've attained ultimate cool. You're a one-person, alien-busting army.

Read John 15:1–6. What do you need God for?

If you could single-handedly spank aliens right out of the galaxy, you'd think you were pretty good. You'd seem ultra-competent. Totally self-sufficient. But get real: You still couldn't get by all by your lonesome. You'd still need a paycheck. Groceries. Electricity from somewhere to charge your laserblaster. And you'd probably sneak your dirty underwear home to Mom to wash.

Next time you think you're independent, put your finger on your belly button and ponder this: Once upon a time, you were tucked inside your mom's tummy, kept alive through a cord.

Nowadays—know it or don't—you're just as dependent. You're designed to draw life from God.

God will never pop you out and shout "Done!" He'll never scissors your spiritual umbilical cord and announce, "Won't be needing that anymore. Might as well knot it off and let it dry up and fall off." You'll never outgrow your spiritual umbilical cord—your connection to God. You're connected to Him like a branch to a vine, and disconnected from Him you can't do *anything*.

Your belly button is a distant memory of physical dependence. And you'll never sprout such a thing as a spiritual belly button. Because you'll never stop needing God.

"I am the vine; you are the branches. If a man remains
in me and I in him, he will bear much fruit;
apart from me you can do nothing."

JOHN 15:5

82

33

WALK ON THE WILD SIDE

Whaddaya mean this wristband will let you track me wherever I go?" Davy quizzed. "What if a bear eats me? Will it still keep beeping in its stomach? Or what if it only eats my arm? How will you find the rest of me?"

"Trust me," was his scoutmaster's reply. "You have your map and compass and know how to use them. You have two days to get to our pick-up spot."

"This map—is it right?" Davy panicked. "Did you check this compass?

"I picked your route carefully. And, yes, that's my best one."

"But there's one more thing," Davy protested. "I've never been where I'm going."

"Davy," his scoutmaster explained, "that's the whole point. Now git!"

Read Genesis 12:1–5. Why trust God?

God told Abram—later called Abraham—where to head to get to the land of His extreme blessings. God's directions were a treasure map Abram trusted enough to leave a comfy life in Ur and go where God had pointed.

God wants to lead you places you've never even thunk of. He's given you a map and compass—His Word, the Bible—that's a hundred percent accurate. It's your total guide to getting along, growing up, and making the most of life.

Trouble is, even if a map is perfect and the path it charts exotically exciting, you'll never move from point A to point B if you don't *trust* the map. You won't ever wholeheartedly follow God if you don't *rely on* the excellence of your outfitter.

You could look at the Christian life and dream up all sorts of reasons *not* to go where God wants you to go: "I'd act more like a Christian if I had more Christian friends." "If I had a deadly illness—then I'd trust God." "Believing God would be easy if I had more time to read my Bible." "I wouldn't do stupid stuff to be popular if I didn't come from such a messed up family." "Being a Christian is easy for pastors—they get paid to do it."

That's making up scary bear stories. God doesn't pass out messed-up maps. He doesn't deal in cracked compasses. He knows how to fend off killer animals.

So be daring. If you believe God, you'll walk on the wild side.

The LORD had said to Abram, "Leave your country, your
people and your father's household and go to the land
I will show you. . . ." So Abram left,
as the LORD had told him.

GENESIS 12:1,4

OPEN DOOR POLICY

"R emember what you said when I was in lock-up?" Steffi asked her youth pastor quietly. "It was right after my attempt. I said, 'How come I'm locked up? They're treating me like I'm a murderer.' You said, 'It's because you tried to hurt Steffi.' "

"You didn't understand me then, did you?" Jason remembered.

"No. I didn't care about Steffi. I didn't know who I was or why I shouldn't hurt myself."

"So has this place helped you? It's got to beat lock-up."

"Yeah. It's taken a few months, but I get what you meant. I don't want to hurt myself ever again. But I'm still stuck on something. I know I'm a Christian. And I know you keep telling me 'God is *always* there for you, Steffi.' But how can God forgive me for how I treated myself—and what I did to my family? My mom is still in pieces. I'm afraid God doesn't want me anywhere near Him."

Read Hebrews 10:19–22. Does God ever get so mad at you He shuts you out?

Picture this. You never get mail, but one day you've get a FedEx envelope at your door. Inside? Membership documents for the poshest club in town—good for a lifetime, all expenses paid. You can't wait! You're gonna golf, swim, smash a racquetball, and twirl in a whirlpool, all on the first day.

You're supposed to get free entry at the front gate. But you're scared. What if the promise was a lie? What if the club secretly votes to boot you out? What if they're just teasing—and want to laugh at you when you show your face?

Most free gifts are scams. But God's offer of friendship is real and irreversible.

Here's why: When Jesus died for your sins, He opened the way for you back to God. If you've said, "Yes, God, I've sinned and need your gift of forgiveness," then you're scrubbed clean, dressed right, fit to talk with the King of the Universe. You can run to the throne of God, the "Most Holy Place" of His presence.

The body of Jesus became a door that's always open. What's up to you is whether you enter in. But if you trust that God has forgiven you, you can talk with Him with absolute confidence— whether you *feel* acceptable or not.

———————————

Let us draw near to God with a sincere heart
in full assurance of faith. . . .

HEBREWS 10:22

ROCKY MOUNTAIN HIGH

You're snowsuited and sunblocked. You stash your rental board in a slot on the gondola and jump inside for your ride to the top of the mountain.

"You know," one of your gondola buddies shares, "an Air Force jet plowed into a lift just like this in Italy. Dropped everybody three or four hundred feet. Twenty people died, and the pilot got off with nothing."

You eye the horizon, hoping to not become the next bowl of fly-by pudding.

The town at the base of the mountain turns tiny. Then it disappears. Before you looms the top half of the mountain you couldn't even see from the bottom.

You exit the gondola and glance around. Never mind that all the signs scream "Beginner." You see a cliff around every curve as you buckle in.

You turn to head downhill. You squeak out one question: "Is this the only way down?"

☛ **Read Psalm 118:6. Can you really trust God to take care of you?**

Life is full of advanced slopes you're not ready to snowboard right now. If you dive down a hill called "Do the Dew" unprepared, you can expect trouble. If you dive too early into life's steep stuff—like a sworn-for-life guy-girl relationship, the mindwarping career-choice thing, or having kids you can't give back when their dad and mom get home—even God's help won't keep you from feeling you're in over your head.

Other slopes—the sinful runs of life—you don't want to 'board at all. True, God forgives. True, God restores. He may be able to retrieve you if you fly off the back side of a mountain. But not even God can scrape you off when you splat yourself to a tree.

There's only one way to get down the mountain of life. When you thrash life with God, you can relax in the protection of the Grand Snowboard Instructor. When you follow God's commands and slice where you're supposed to, you can be sure you're hanging right next to Him. You might be shocked when He challenges you. You might not realize you're ready when He shoots you down the steep runs. You might not even enjoy the whole hill. But you'll survive with a smile.

If all of life were easy, you wouldn't need to trust your Instructor. But if you're sure God protects you, you fear nothing.

———————

The LORD is with me; I will not be afraid.

PSALM 118:6

HANGING IN

Almost a foot shorter than anyone else in his grade, Brian lives with a long and ugly *can't-do-that* list.

He can't reach the pull-up bar.

He can't come close to spiking a volleyball.

He can't dream of looking a classmate in the eye.

He can't reach half the bookshelves in the library.

He can't see the blackboard unless he sits in the front row.

He can't stand getting laughed at in the locker room.

Trapped in the body of a lot-younger kid, Brian can't make himself grow. He can't change his situation. But he can choose to conquer it.

📖 **Read Hebrews 12:4–11. What keeps life's tough stuff from being a waste?**

If pain were pointless, people wouldn't beat their bodies in workout rooms or do waddle-till-they-wheeze marathons to stay fit. Adultish-types wouldn't willingly pull all-nighters to survive college, work graveyard shifts to save for a house, stay glued together in nasty marriages to jumpstart love, or give up money to help people they've never met.

Painful Truth #1: You can choose pain to gain huge prizes.

Painful Truth #2: You can choose to find gain even in pain you don't pick.

No circumstance of your life outsmarts God's control. He can rearrange pain or remove it. But if He doesn't shoo away the troubles that tromp through your life, count those troubles as part of God's training to make you like Him.

Pain only works its wonders if you submit to its training. When you accept as part of God's discipline the hardships that strike out of nowhere and slap you upside the head, He makes them into something useful. They'll make you righteous and peaceful. And they'll remind you that you're truly God's daughter or son.

If you try to wiggle free from the weights in God's gym, though, what's supposed to be your spiritual workout is a waste—it just wastes *you*, that is. It becomes stupid suffering, not a sweaty workout for your soul.

If you understand that tough times are God's discipline, you'll learn from what you can't change.

No discipline seems pleasant at the time, but painful. Later on, however, it produces a harvest of righteousness and peace for those who have been trained by it.

HEBREWS 12:11

MISS SNOTDAUGHTER'S NERD COLLECTION

Miss Snotdaughter," a member of the talent show committee finally says, "we want to make sure we understand you correctly. You're auditioning this group because they do *not* have talent?"

"Exactly!" Jaye Snotdaughter squeals. "It's really *my* talent on display. I'm a nerd collector. And this simply is the best set of nerds I've ever assembled."

"For starters," Jaye chirps, "take Belinda. She's quite ugly. Everyone says so.

"And Charles has a lisp," she continues. "Say something, Charles."

"Hi. I'm Charelth." Jaye beams.

"Jaqi just moved here from out of state," Jaye pouts. "She has no friends at all.

"Then there's Riley. He's in seventh grade, but I can already tell he'll *never* get a girlfriend. He's really a fine specimen. He'll be with me a long time.

"And Ben's just flunking math," Jaye finishes. "I'll help him raise his grade, then throw him back. He's kind of a temporary nerd. He rounds out my collection nicely, don't you think?"

☑ Read 1 John 4:19–21. What gives us the power to love people we don't like?

God could treat us like His nerd collection. After all, in our unforgiven and unfixed state we're pretty repulsive (Romans 3:10–18). And if our good points are dung—like Paul says in Philippians 3:8—then the bad stuff we do is Ultrasauraus doo. It takes a house-size pooper scooper to clean up after us.

Despite our failings, God doesn't put you and the rest of your species on display in a loser zoo. He sees something special in you, because He made you (Psalm 100:3). Nothing can separate you from His love (Romans 8:38–39), which reaches to the heavens (Psalm 36:5). And don't forget this: God's colossal love for you and your fellow earthlings is why He sent His Son, Jesus, to live and die (John 3:16).

If God had wanted you to make pets of the less-than-likable people around you, He would have built them with collars. Seeing none, it's obvious He wants you to do more than collect nerds. He wants you to love them with the love He lavishes on you.

When you know God loves you, you love others.

We love because he first loved us.

1 JOHN 4:19

BOMB SQUAD

When Aimee sat down in front of Scott at the school musical—smack where he could stare at her while pretending to study the stage—his heart climbed into his throat and choked him. *An hour and a half*, he gargled, *of watching my sweets watch the show.*

God—thanks to a blunt youth pastor—had taught Scott the Bible's principles about guy-girl stuff: Control yourself (1 Thessalonians 4:3–5). Keep your thoughts clean (Matthew 5:28). Sex is for marriage (Hebrews 13:4). And don't hook yourself to non-Christians, for a long time or little (2 Corinthians 6:14).

Weird thing: Once Scott even thought he'd heard God say, "Don't go near her."

Thanks, God, his thoughts sassed back. *You didn't have to say that. She looks at me like I look at meatloaf in the cafeteria. I can't get near her.*

Flash forward a few months. Everyone finds out what Aimee had hidden for a long time: Her friends had pulled her into a serious drinking habit. And that had led to a lot of other ugly situations. Scott felt sorry for her. But suddenly he was also glad he hadn't gotten her as his girl.

✔ Read Psalm 19:7–11. Why obey God?

It seemed like a strange game. Each day a total stranger sent you a tiny electronics gizmo and some assembly directions in the mail. Day by day, piece by piece, you were supposed to put the parts together. One day—when you've followed the final steps—you wake up. You've got a bomb taped to your chest. Turns out the parts and directions came from an enemy. The bomb ticks, ready to explode, you're not sure when.

Life's like that. It blows up in your face when you follow the wrong directions. It explodes when you want what God says you can't have.

Good thing: God is head of the bomb squad, and He keeps you from detonating your life in a couple ways. Sometimes He arranges your circumstances to keep harm out of your life, not letting you near things you don't even know you shouldn't want.

God has also given you the Bible. His commands are like instructions for defusing a bomb—or for spotting one as it's being built. His rules steer you toward life and away from stupid, unnecessary pain (John 10:10).

And if you trust that God wants what's best for you, you follow His good instructions.

The statutes of the LORD are trustworthy, making wise the simple. . . . By them is your servant warned;
in keeping them there is great reward."

PSALM 19:7,11

BUSTING LOOSE

Mom and Dad," Trent confessed, "I'm sorry."

The umpteen other times Trent had gone on a church retreat he'd listened to the youth pastor's Bible talks and figured they were for the kids next to him wearing the Grateful Dead T-shirts. God, he figured, was rapping on *their* heads, not his.

This time, though, God took a wrecking ball to Trent, knocking some spiritual sense into him. He felt shock waves rumble through as he recognized his Sunday school snottery—how he thought he was better than other people, how he had a mighty swirly potty mouth, how at home he'd been on a six-month rampage about homework and chores, and how his sneaking out of the house had betrayed his parents.

When he got home to talk to his mom and dad, it all dumped out again.

"Hey, tough guy," his dad said, trying to brush the sorrys aside. "It's okay."

"No, Dad, it's not okay," Trent persisted. "I've been hurting *me*. I've been hurting *you*. And I don't want to be that way any-more."

👉 Read Ephesians 4:22–24. Why does God want to change us?

You can have a pretty sad day—or year—when you start to realize how bad sin is. The Psalms say it well: "Some sat in darkness and the deepest gloom, prisoners suffering in iron chains, for they had rebelled against the words of God and despised the counsel of the Most High" (107:10–11). All sin puts you in chains, even if you don't take your sin seriously, even if you don't recognize your bondage.

God's goal is to set you free. Listen again to the Psalm: "He [God] brought them out of darkness and the deepest gloom and broke away their chains. Let them give thanks to the LORD for his unfailing love and his wonderful deeds. . . ." (107:14–15).

Sin is like two chains. Saying "yes" to God's offer of forgiveness in Jesus sets you free from the *penalty* of sin. But there's a second chain: the *power* of sin. You maybe know about God's forgiveness. He also wants you to experience His freedom.

Sin hurts. But breaking that second chain starts with knowing you need to get free. When you know sin enchains you, you let God cut you loose.

You were taught, with regard to your former way of life, to put off your old self, which is being corrupted by its deceitful desires . . . and to put on the new self.

EPHESIANS 4:22, 24

BOBBING
HEADS

You *doh-on't ski-ee, you doh-on't ski-ee.* With the taunts of her shrimpy six-year-old cousins reverbing in her ears since the last family reunion, Teresa wasn't going to let this chance to learn to water-ski escape.

"Teresa," her dad said seriously, "you've got two rules to follow when—er, *if* you fall. First, let go of the rope—or you'll get dragged and get a snootful of water. Second, poke a ski up out of the water—it helps boats see you."

When Teresa wiped out, she forgot the rules. She gulped water. She thought about what might be living in the deep end of the lake and flailed wildly for help.

Back in the boat, she shook. She coughed.

But she felt safe. And she wanted to try again.

✔ Read Hebrews 13:5–6. What helps you try tough stuff?

You might fall and torque your head. You might burn your legs on the tow rope. But bodyslaps and waterswallows are usually the worst part of water-skiing wipeouts. Except for one possibility: You don't want to get mowed over by a boat.

You want to get your ski up to signal for help.

God watches over you as you slalom through life, always ready to help. He's quick to swing the boat around and pick you up when you wipe.

God wants you to push, to dare, to try bold, new stuff. And He promises that you'll never face a situation too big: "You can trust God, who will not permit you to be tempted more than you can stand. But when you are tempted, he will also give you a way to escape so that you will be able to stand it" (1 Corinthians 10:13, NCV).

That verse isn't just about urges to have evil sex, do drugs, or chant rock and roll. It also fits temptations to despair, to throw pity parties, and to give up. The verse right before warns to never imagine you can rely solely on yourself. The verse right after cautions against depending on anything other than God. The writer of the verses you read in Hebrews says the same thing: You can face anything if you face it with God.

When you know God is always with you, you're willing to try hard stuff.

God has said, "Never will I leave you; never will I forsake you."
So we say with confidence, "The Lord is my helper;
I will not be afraid."

HEBREWS 13:5–6

NO MORE STINKY DAYS

Your day stinks from the start.

As soon as you sweep into school, you get shook down for your lunch money. Then you do dismally on a pop quiz. You get whacked in the jaw in gym.

When you arrive home, your day gets worse.

Your dad doesn't like the mess in your room. You run out the door mad. You step where you shouldn't. You squish. "YEEEEUCK!" you scream. And without thinking, you do the one thing you could possibly do to make the stink worse: You wipe your bare feet on the kitchen rug. Your dad glares. Your brother gags.

"MOMMMM . . ." you wail. "NOBODY LIKES ME!"

"Well," she says calmly, "you do smell like dog poop."

☛ **Read Revelation 5:6–14. Does God guarantee people will like you?**

You can get lost in the seals and bowls and thunder and trumpets of the Bible book of Revelation. But what you just read is

99

unmistakably clear: God is building a people who belong to Him, a gaggle of friends who rely on His care now and forever.

There's a crowd of people following God.

Any no good, very bad, horrible day will leave you feeling friendless. Everybody faces those days. But being a Christian might make your lonely days feel even lonelier. You get left out for making right choices in your quest to follow God.

Jesus has a promise: He said that anyone who leaves "home or brothers or sisters or mother or father or children or fields for me and the gospel" will receive "a hundred times" as much in "this present age" and "in the age to come, eternal life" (Mark 10:29–30).

If God rewards leaving fields for His sake, He for sure cares when following Him means you lose friends. And Revelation pictures a whopper way God keeps His promise: Heaven will be full of people from every tribe and nation.

They're here. Right around you. Right now. What Jesus said means you'll see some of those new friends soon, in "this present age." And Revelation shows you'll also be hanging with a cool crowd for all eternity.

If you follow God, you'll have friends forever.

———————

"With your blood you purchased men for God from every tribe and language and people and nation. You have made them to be a kingdom and priests to serve our God. . . ."

REVELATION 5:9–10

100

ACKNOWLEDGMENTS

A hearty thanks to Rochelle Glöege, Natasha Sperling, Janna Anderson, and Cathy Engstrom for their tender care of my books.

A warm thanks to Gary and Carol Johnson, for making a spot for me at Bethany House Publishers and allowing me to pursue God's dreams.

And a tender thanks to my wife—Lyn—and kiddies—Nate, Karin, and Elise—for being ever faithful and fun. Thanks for letting me write.

INDEX

Looking for something specific about popularity bubbles and peer fear? For each reading in *Was That a Balloon or Did Your Head Just Pop?* here's a one-liner description, the Scripture used, and a memory jogger summarizing the Scripture.

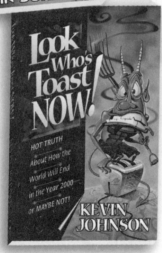